# Baby and Beyond

## Progression in Play for Babies and Children

## The Natural World

Published 2009 by A&C Black Publishers Limited
36 Soho Square, London W1D 3QY
www.acblack.com

First published 2006 by Featherstone Education Limited
ISBN 978-1-9050-1957-1

Text © Liz Williams and Sally Featherstone 2006
Illustrations © Martha Hardy 2006
A CIP record for this publication is available from the British Library.

**To see our full range of titles
visit www.acblack.com**

# Contents

# Baby and Beyond

## A series of books for practitioners working with children from birth to five and beyond

This book gives ideas for introducing and extending role play activities and experiences for babies and young children. Each page spread contains a range of experiences and a selection of ideas for each of the developmental stages of the Early Years Foundation Stage (EYFS). We have retained the descriptive names of the four earlier developmental stages from Birth to Three Matters, while adjusting the age ranges to cover the whole EYFS:

| Birth - 11 months | 8 - 20 months | 16 - 26 months | 22 - 40 months | 40 - 60+ months |
| --- | --- | --- | --- | --- |
| Development Stage 1 | Development Stage 2 | Development Stage 3 | Development Stages 4 and 5 | Development Stages 5 and 6 |

## Introduction

Experiences of the natural world are essential elements in all Early Years settings. The experiences help babies and children to look and listen, to touch and feel, and to enjoy being out of doors. As children grow older, outdoor play gives a firm foundation to the use of tools, investigation of materials, and knowledge and understanding of weather, seasons and living things in the world around them. The activities described in this book are all appropriate to children from birth to five (and beyond) and we have linked them to the developmental stages of the curriculum guidance for Birth to Three and the Foundation Stage (soon to become the Early Years Foundation Stage).

Babies and children also need the company and stimulation of knowledgeable and interested adults if they are to extend their play into thinking and learning. Adult/child interaction is essential at all levels to encourage children's language, learning and development. Talking with and listening to babies and children is also vital in supporting and developing self-esteem. Observing their play, both indoors and in the garden or outside area, is essential for recognising both their achievements and their needs, so you can plan for future learning.

As babies and children move through the developmental stages, experiences can be offered in differing ways and at different working heights - lying down, sitting (both propped and independent), kneeling or standing - and some children will develop preferences. Some older children will still enjoy working lying down, while some very young children will be determined to sit or stand even before they are able to do it alone! Using small and large trays (such as plant and builders' trays) are simple but effective ways to enable easy access for all babies and children. Young babies need to have access to the experiences at floor level, on an adult's knee and in their arms, so you will need to plan for all these. It is also essential to provide activities both indoors and in the garden, each giving an added dimension to the simple resources you offer.

The experiences of the natural world described in this book encourage development and learning through sensory play in the natural world. They all use sight, touch and smell, and of course, many babies and children will want to taste the experience as well! Enhancing experiences in different ways will expand the use of all senses, for example by focusing on colours, textures and sounds. Most babies and children actually learn better in a garden, and many of the experiences are free! Providing the babies and children are suitably dressed and warm enough, they (and you) can and should go out in all weathers! Little outings for babies and wet splashing for older children are essential for learning as well as for their health and wellbeing. Try to ensure that the children in your care are out of doors every day, whatever the weather.

Involving children in the preparation and clearing up of activities is also part of the learning and the fun. Even very young children can help with simple preparation tasks, and as they become more confident and independent, they can begin to select their own materials and resources, explore the garden on their own, do digging and other gardening activities, watch birds and minibeasts and explore surfaces and materials. Planning and preparing for the activity is often as enjoyable as playing with what you have prepared - and of course, if children help with preparation, they also know where to put the things when they have finished with them and can get them when they need them!

Your planning of the experiences in this book will take account of your observations of children's play and current interests, their current stage of development (not just their age) and the need to offer a wide range of natural experiences over the child's time with you. These progressions will help you to plan an appropriate range of experiences, and by suggesting additions and new stimuli as children's needs and abilities develop, you can ensure that the activities are fresh and exciting each time you offer them.

Sally Featherstone, Liz Williams; 2006

| 0-11 months | 8-20 months | 16 - 26 months | 22 - 40 months | 40 - 60+ months |

| Development Stage 1 | Development Stage 2 | Development Stage 3 | Development Stages 4 and 5 | Development Stages 5 and 6 |

### Leaf

Leaves are a free and ever changing resource for you and the children. Leaves are varied, tactile, endless in shape, size and texture and change with the seasons.

Make sure that the leaves you use are safe for babies and children to handle.

## Young babies (0-11 months)

Take babies into the garden with you and hold them as they look at, touch and feel growing leaves on trees and bushes.

Pick a leaf and use it to gently stroke the baby's arms, hands and cheeks. Let them stroke your hand or cheek in return. This short activity can be undertaken quickly and needs no preparation, so take babies outside for simple little explorations of this sort in all weathers, seasons and at all times of day.

### Development Stage 1

## Babies (8-20 months)

When you are in the garden, sometimes pick a leaf to explore with a young baby. Talk about how it feels, stroke it with your hands and fingers, wave, pat and poke a leaf. Do this in Spring and Autumn as well for a different feel. Float some small leaves in a bowl or tray of water, or freeze some in ice cubes. Be with a sitting baby in a baby chair or stroller, under a tree or bush or other 'leafy place' for a while. Look up at the leaves and the shadows they make.

### Development Stage 2

## Young children (16-26 months)

 Collect some leaves and make the simplest of mobiles by threading them on wool. Float leaves in water trays, set them in jelly or hide them in foam or gloop. Continue to collect fallen leaves and explore their features. Talk about soft, smooth, rough, prickly, tickly, hairy. Enjoy scuffing in fallen leaves at the park or in your garden. Look up at the sun or clouds through leaves to see the patterns they make.

### Development Stage 3

## Children (22-40 months)

Collect fallen autumn leaves and make a collage by sticking  them with white glue all over an opened-out bin liner. Try to cover the whole surface, and overlap the leaves. Paint the surface of your collage with a coat of dilute white glue and wait for it to dry. Now carefully peel the sheet of leaves off the plastic backing to see a lovely hanging of transparent leaves. Hang this against a window or in front of a light to get the best effect.

### Development Stages 4 and 5

## Older Children (40-60+ months)

Make leaf prints and rubbings, cut them out and make your own tree. Get a big cardboard tube and hang the leaves from branches of card. Or make ice hangings. Arrange small twigs of evergreen leaves and holly, holly berries and some sequins in shallow containers (lids, tins, trays). Add a loop of ribbon or string and fill the container with water. Freeze them, pop the hangings out of the container and hang them up outside.

### Development Stages 5 and 6

## Flower

If you haven't got any flowers in the garden of your setting, get the children to help you to plant some. Try to plant flowers for all seasons of the year, and include some perennials and winter flowering varieties. Check that the flowers you plant are safe for children - The Little Book of Growing Things has lots of ideas.

## Young babies (0-11 months)

Walk round your garden, the park or a local florist's shop and look at the flowers together. Babies love holding flowers - holding a daisy, buttercup or other single flower is a good way to develop grip, and looking at it will encourage wrist action and visual focus. Talk about the flower as they or you hold it. Make sure it is in their focus (between 8/15 inches/20-25 cm away). Put some pot pourri in little fabric bags for babies to feel.

### Development Stage 1

## Babies (8-20 months)

Put sitting and crawling babies on lawns and other grass so they can explore buttercups and daisies. Put strollers and baby chairs near flower borders and tubs where the babies can see and touch individual flowers. Put individual flowers in plastic pockets for patting and looking at. Have flowers in your setting - make it a priority to always have natural things for children to see and handle.
Talk about how the flowers feel and smell.

### Development Stage 2

### Young children (16-26 months)

Look for flowers as you go on walks and visits. Stop and look at shops, petrol stations, gardens, parks, markets and flower displays. Take the children in small groups to visit a local florist or garden centre. Make the visit more interesting by buying something to take back to your setting - a packet of seeds, a pansy or primula in pot, a bunch of daffodils. Look at these when you return to your setting, using the language of shape, colour perfume and size.

**Development Stage 3**

### Children (22-40 months)

Find and cut out pictures of flowers from magazines and catalogues. Use the flower pictures to make a big collage of all the different sorts. Get a few seedlings or cheap bedding plants and help the children to plant them in pots, tubs or flower beds. Plant flower seeds or seedlings of fast growing varieties such as sunflowers, Russian vine or Morning Glory; or plant some perfumed varieties - sweet peas, lavender or herbs.

**Development Stages 4 and 5**

### Older Children (40-60+ months)

Order some spring bulbs from a catalogue and plant them in bulb fibre or in the garden. Remember to have the picture of the flower available when the bulb is planted! Try a novel way of pressing flowers - let the children arrange flowers and petals on the sticky side of a small piece of sticky-backed plastic. Cover with another piece of plastic to make a sandwich. Make a hole in the top and hang in a window or make several into a mobile.

**Development Stages 5 and 6**

## Pebble and stone

Pebbles, stones and rocks of all sorts are a lovely addition to gardens and outdoor areas. You can buy a huge range of these from garden centres and builders' merchants. Have polished and natural types and plenty of containers for collecting and carrying. Children need to be <u>taught</u> how to handle these materials safely and carefully.

## Young babies (0-11 months)

Start with just one smooth, round, clean pebble, big enough for a baby to see and hold (and too big to swallow!). Add stones and pebbles to treasure baskets for indoor and outdoor play.
Pick up stones and pebbles as you walk in the park, the field or the garden. Look at these and talk to the baby about their shape, colour, texture. Bring a stone back from a walk and put it near the changing area to remind you and the babies of your outings.

### Development Stage 1

## Babies (8-20 months)

Offer bowls and baskets of smooth stones for handling and grasping to strengthen fingers and hands. Add smooth tins and boxes to drop stones in for an 'in and out' posting game. Show babies how to bang two manageable pebbles together as a first musical instrument. Put a few glass pebbles and a small amount of coloured water in a small plastic jar. Fix the lid on securely for a fascinating rattling toy. Set pebbles in concrete in your garden for sensory crawling.

### Development Stage 2

## Young children (16-26 months)

Add smooth stones and pebbles to water trays and bowls of coloured water. Make a simple, safe water feature with water bubbling over pebbles and stones. Paint pebbles with thick brushes and bright colours. Set these in a path or just place them around your garden. Offer shingle or gravel as a change from sand. Put it in shallow trays or 'Tuff Spots' and offer shovels and buckets for scooping or diggers for driving.

### Development Stage 3

## Children (22-40 months)

Get a bag of cobbles or big pebbles from a garden centre and offer them for shifting and tipping in barrows and buckets.
Use patterned or plain table mats or shallow trays of sand with glass pebbles for making patterns and pictures.
Collect a few pebbles from a seaside visit and set up a small world rock pool with blue water, small world sea creatures. Add plastic strips and shapes for seaweed and fish.

### Development Stages 4 and 5

## Older Children (40-60+ months)

Collect some pizza boxes and some pebbles, shells and stones. Fill the pizza boxes with ready mixed cement (adult only), then let the children push stones and other objects into the wet cement. When dry, remove the box and you have a natural collage to mount on an outside wall or even set into a path. Use fine brushes or permanent markers to draw faces or figures on smooth pebbles. Make them into a wall decoration by pushing into concrete.

### Development Stages 5 and 6

## Shell

Shells are another great free resource, just as varied and fascinating a stones to feel and examine. Most are tough enough for the wear and tear that babies and children will give them, but watch for splintering and sharp edges. Try bargain shops for bags of decorative shells and polished pebbles.

## Young babies (0-11 months)

Look for shells at the beach, in the garden, in charity and pound shops. Ask parents and children to bring them from home and holidays.

Add a very big shell to a treasure basket for a new experience. Sit together and hold a shell, talking about its texture, colour and weight. Listen for the sea by holding it to your ear, then to the baby's ear - talk about what you hear.

### Development Stage 1

## Babies (8-20 months)

Add big shells to treasure baskets - babies love having heavy objects as well as light ones.

Slide shells down cardboard tubes and guttering or drop them in water. Bury a shell or two in a bowl of sand and let the baby uncover them. Put a few shells in a box or tin with a lid to make a rattle for shaking and banging. Hide a shell in a feely bag or cover it with a piece of thin fabric for the baby to find or uncover.

### Development Stage 2

## Young children (16-26 months)

Add shells to the tools available for pressing into dough or clay. Or dip them in paint for printing. Offer collections of shells for sorting and handling; add some tins and boxes for added fun.

Offer shells for pattern making in shallow trays of sand or clay. Put them in water trays or hide them in gloop or slime. Hang some shells on strings by using 'Hard as Nails' glue and make your own shell wind chimes or instruments.

### Development Stage 3

## Children (22-40 months)

Collect some snails from the garden, and make a snail home in a plastic aquarium. Put some soil and leaves in the bottom and add some lettuce leaves for them to eat. Put a sheet of glass or plastic over the top or they will escape! Offer the children magnifying glasses to watch the snails, particularly as they move across the sides of the aquarium. Talk about how they move, eat, see and hear. Let them go where you found them.

### Development Stages 4 and 5

## Older Children (40-60+ months)

Find out about the creatures that live in shells - not just the permanent owners, but how other creatures take over empty shells. Read 'Sharing a Shell' or 'Sally and the Limpet'. Talk about different sorts of shells. Explore their shapes - spirals, fans, pairs, 'slipper' shapes; their textures - smooth, ridged, shiny, pearl; their colours and patterns. Encourage children to bring a shell or two back from seaside holidays to add to a collection. Make shell pictures and patterns.

### Development Stages 5 and 6

15

## Seed

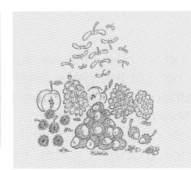

Seeds offer a wide range of opportunities for exploration, craft and shape/size work. Don't forget the fresh and dried seeds we eat, and the seeds in fruit, nuts and vegetables.

Take care with dried peas and beans - children may be tempted to put them in nostrils and ears! Check the berries that grow in your garden to make sure they are safe.

## Young babies (0-11 months)

When you are walking or sitting in the garden or park, look out for berries, seeds and nuts on plants, bushes and trees. Take babies close to these, so they can see them too. Talk about them, feel them if they can be reached, look at the shapes, colours and textures. Don't worry if you don't know what they are called, just encourage babies to look and explore the world with you. Collect conkers or other big seeds to take back with you.

### Development Stage 1

## Babies (8-20 months)

If you sit with them to ensure they don't swallow any, babies can have conkers, big dried beans, acorns and other big seeds for handling, posting into boxes and tins, sliding down slopes and burying in sand. They will also love looking at seeds 'captured' in little zip lock bags to keep them safe and dry. When you go on seasonal walks, show babies how dandelion seeds float, how sycamore seeds spin, how acorns sit in a little cup.

### Development Stage 2

## Young children (16-26 months)

Offer young children dried seeds (beans, peas, lentils) for 'cooking' and mixing in bowls and pans with wooden spoons. Try a tray of grass seed as an alternative to sand - it behaves very differently as the children scoop it with hands and scoops. Look for seeds in fruit and vegetables - apple and orange pips, bean and pea seeds, even banana seeds. Try washing the seeds from a water-melon or a marrow, and use them to make necklaces.

**Development Stage 3**

## Children (22-40 months)

Plant some quick growing seeds such as grass seeds, mustard and cress or beans and watch them each day as they grow. Talk about what is happening and what the seeds need to make them grow into plants. Plant some beans or sweet peas outside in a 'wigwam' of canes to make a living den which produces food!
Offer big quantities of dry beans, rice and pulses for play with scoops and paper bags to develop fine motor skills.

**Development Stages 4 and 5**

## Older Children (40-60+ months)

Collect seeds from snack fruit and familiar vegetables and try growing them - try avocado stones, orange /lemon/grapefruit pips, melon or tomato seeds. Go on a walk to collect Autumn seeds and try growing conkers, acorns, nuts, hips and haws. Or use the seeds to make collages, mobiles or structures with twigs and leaves. Talk about the animals that eat seeds and how they store them for the winter. Read some stories about seeds.

**Development Stages 5 and 6**

## Minibeast

Keeping a range of pets in your setting may be complicated, but experiencing living things is an important part of early years experience. Minibeasts can make a valuable contribution to this part of children's experiences, and they come uninvited. Don't miss any chance, however squeamish you might be - children love minibeasts!

## Young babies (0-11 months)

When you are with young babies, draw their attention to spider webs, ants, flies, bees, butterflies and other minibeasts as you walk around your garden or park. Many minibeasts move too fast for baby focus, so hold a ladybird on your hand so they can see it, watch a caterpillar climb up a leaf, or a snail slither across a wet path. Put a beetle or a small spider in a clear container for a few minutes so they can see what it is like.

### Development Stage 1

## Babies (8-20 months)

Continue to use small containers to protect bugs and small creatures from babies' close attention and developing hand control! Get a spider catcher or bug box and use this to trap ants, beetles, spiders, ladybirds or woodlice for a short period. Don't forget to release them in the place where you found them - and try not to show any fear or resistance YOU may feel for 'creepy crawlies' - children are fascinated by them!

### Development Stage 2

## Young children (16-26 months)

Continue to catch small creatures with the children, teaching them the importance of careful handling of minibeasts and returning them to the same place in the garden when they have had a look. Try putting a piece of guttering or an old bucket in a corner of the garden and lifting it gently after a day or two to see what you have found! Extend your range by finding snails (and slugs) to watch for a few minutes. Watch ants, butterflies, bees and flies in the garden.

### Development Stage 3

## Children (22-40 months)

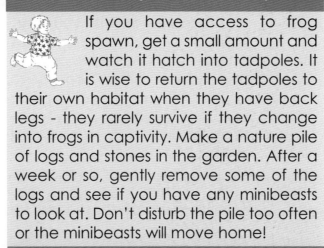

If you have access to frog spawn, get a small amount and watch it hatch into tadpoles. It is wise to return the tadpoles to their own habitat when they have back legs - they rarely survive if they change into frogs in captivity. Make a nature pile of logs and stones in the garden. After a week or so, gently remove some of the logs and see if you have any minibeasts to look at. Don't disturb the pile too often or the minibeasts will move home!

### Development Stages 4 and 5

## Older Children (40-60+ months)

Snails are more robust pets for young children, as long as they have some tasty leaves to eat and a dark place to hide at night. You could also make a simple wormery in a tall jar of soil with layers of leaves and sand. Add a few worms and cover the jar with black paper. Remove the paper after a few days and you should see how the worms have mixed the sand, leaves and soil together.
Send for a butterfly box from www.greengardener.co.uk

### Development Stages 5 and 6

19

## Bird

Birds are everywhere. Wherever you work, you can attract birds to your setting and enjoy their company. Children will soon begin to recognise different birds and to remember their needs - and watching birds from indoors and outside is a very good way to practice concentrating and sitting still!

## Young babies (0-11 months)

When you are with your key babies, sit by the window and watch birds flying and on the ground. Young babies may find that birds move too quickly for their young eyes, so fit a bird feeder to the outside of the window to encourage the birds to stay longer and closer.

Bigger birds such as ducks and swans are easier to see, so take some food and walk to the park to watch these birds up close.

### Development Stage 1

## Babies (8-20 months)

Go on frequent walks to ponds and other places where birds live and feed. These could be sparrows, pigeons, ducks, geese or swans. Sit and look for a while at what the birds are doing (you don't need to take food, this will sometimes result in more birds that you need!). Make sure you have a bird table in your setting and that you feed the birds regularly with a variety of food. Some bird feeders stick to the outside of windows. Put them low down where babies can see them.

### Development Stage 2

## Young children (16-26 months)

Make or buy a simple bird bath and wait for the birds to come for a drink or bath. You can make simple bird feeders from plastic bottles with holes cut in them, or a hanging feeder from a pie dish suspended from three strings. Make several different feeders and put them in different places round the garden. Be aware of cats and other predators, and clean the feeders and baths regularly (an adult only job!).

**Development Stage 3**

## Children (22-40 months)

Make bird cake by mixing seeds and nuts in a bowl and adding some melted fat (not too hot!). Stir well and pack into plastic pots. Before it hardens, push a string into the mixture, so you can hang the bird cake from a branch or hook.

Talk about nests and eggs and read some egg books such as 'Hatch Egg, Hatch', 'Horton Hatches the Egg', or 'Chicken to Egg'. Investigate mothers and babies or read 'Owl Babies'.

**Development Stages 4 and 5**

## Older Children (40-60+ months)

Older children can become bird spotters, recording the numbers and even the types of birds they see in your garden. Help them by setting up quiet places near windows or outside so they can watch birds. Offer some binoculars and bird spotting books. Talk about eggs, look at a chicken's egg in detail, inside as well as outside. Try to get some duck, goose or quail eggs for comparison of size, shape and colour. Get an incubator and hatch some duck or chicken eggs in your setting.

**Development Stages 5 and 6**

## Water

Water plays such a big part in our lives - from the smallest puddle to the biggest lake or sea. Children of all ages are drawn to water and love playing with it in all its forms. Don't forget ice!

Always supervise children carefully near water. Even shallow water is a danger!

## Young babies (0-11 months)

Make sure they are well protected in waterproof clothing and take babies out of doors for short periods on rainy days when it's not too cold. Hold hands and faces up to feel the rain, explore how it runs down clothing and skin, look at raindrops in puddles and on windows.
Even babies who can't yet walk love to be held while they splash or paddle in a puddle, stream or shallow pond.

**Development Stage 1**

## Babies (8-20 months)

Warm water and bubbles are a lovely experience for babies. Try shallow water and bubble bath in a builder's tray or another shallow container. Stay close as they will be slippery! Or put some food colouring in water for simple splashing and patting without the bubbles.
As soon as babies can stand with help, begin to explore rain and the puddles it makes. Hold their hands or support them in standing so they can splash and stamp in wet paths and in shallow puddles.

**Development Stage 2**

## Young children (16-26 months)

 Invest in some waterproof clothing, boots and umbrellas so young children can continue to explore rain and puddles. Let them splash and stamp in wet weather, or ride trikes through shallow water. In summer, use the same clothing to protect them from hoses and sprinklers on grass or patios. Water trays should be permanent features of your setting, with varied equipment to use in them, coloured water, ice and other additions.

### Development Stage 3

## Children (22-40 months)

Make sure you offer plenty of different sorts of equipment and tools for water play. Store them in containers near the water tray, and check regularly to ensure that the water tray does not get too full of equipment. Put a board across the end of the tray so children can put objects aside for a time. Offer containers, boats, water wheels, sieves, funnels, tubing, plastic syringes, pipettes, plastic bottles and jars - but not all at once!!

### Development Stages 4 and 5

## Older Children (40-60+ months)

Offer brushes and buckets of water for outdoor water 'painting' or use windscreen scrapers and sprays for spraying and cleaning windows. Wash the wheeled toys using watering cans and hoses, brush water from puddles with small brooms and brushes. Make and melt ice shapes and float some of these in the water tray. Talk about the uses of water and how important it is in the lives of plants, animals and people.

### Development Stages 5 and 6

23

## Mud

Mud in all its forms is available and exciting to children. It was one of the first playthings! Make sure children wash their hands well after playing with mud, but remember that in most places, mud is safe. If you are unsure, use a bag of soil based compost from a garden centre - this will be sterilised and safe to use.

## Young babies (0-11 months)

Babies are always intent on trying everything with their mouths, so you should watch carefully even with sterilised soil. However, babies should not be excluded from this activity! Mixing, patting, poking with a finger are all little experiences that babies can manage and will enjoy. Holding a baby so their feet can just paddle in fairly liquid mud will be something most of them will love - and it will sensitise their feet ready for standing and walking.

**Development Stage 1**

## Babies (8-20 months)

As soon as babies can stand (either with or without help) help them to explore mud, either by walking in it in the garden or exploring a tray of it on the floor or on a low table. You could sit a baby in a builder's tray of liquid mud for really messy play, or offer them a shallow layer of mud in a big tray to trail their fingers in. Patting lumps of mud, poking fingers in wet, damp and dry soil are all of great interest to children at this stage.

**Development Stage 2**

## Young children (16-26 months)

Try very liquid mud in pots with thick brushes or foam dabbers for painting on surfaces outside - it will wash off easily with a hose (or just wait for the rain). At this stage children will love painting anything - small world animals, plastic bricks, wheeled toys, toy cars, even dolls (undressed of course!). When they have finished, offer bubbly warm water or a trickling hose to help with washing the mud off again.

**Development Stage 3**

## Children (22-40 months)

Fill a sand or water tray with compost or soil. Add some patty pans, sand moulds and spoons for filling and emptying, and making mud pies. Put the tray on the ground and add some small boards or plastic table mats for putting the pies on. Old teeshirts, cotton shirts or fabric aprons make working on the ground easier than stiff plastic aprons! Try a thin layer of wet mud in a builder's tray for track making with toy cars and lorries.

**Development Stages 4 and 5**

## Older Children (40-60+ months)

Use liquid mud for sponge or other printing - try kitchen implements, feathers, leaves, toothbrushes etc. Or dip cars in it and make tracks and trails. Bury objects such as marbles, beads, coins, small world animals or glass beads in <u>dry</u> compost for a great sieving or digging hunt. Create a digging area in your  garden where children can just dig - no planting, just digging with child sized spades, rakes, trowels and hoes. Try the Internet, DIY stores or educational suppliers for children's garden tools.

**Development Stages 5 and 6**

## Air and wind

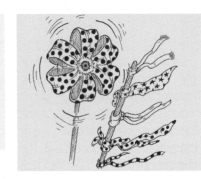

Explore the way invisible air feels and behaves. Start by just letting young babies experience the unusual feeling of air moving across their skin and hair. Explore air and wind indoors and out, experiment with what it can do and how we use its power. Make and find toys and other things that are powered by air or wind - and don't forget the effect of wind on weather.

## Young babies (0-11 months)

Just being held in a summer breeze and feeling it on their face will stimulate most babies to shiver, smile or otherwise show reactions of pleasure or displeasure.

Use hand fans to blow air gently onto legs, arms and hands or hair (not faces). Hang up mobiles that move in a breeze - use feathers, shiny CDs, ribbons, leaves, or unbreakable Christmas decorations. Put them over radiators, near windows or in other places where they will move in the breeze.

### Development Stage 1

## Babies (8-20 months)

Attach simple windmills, streamers and other wind toys to pushchairs, window catches, bushes and trees. Babies love the whirr and flutter of wind blown toys.

Stand or sit with them and watch clouds racing on a windy day or making shadows in the sun. Explore blowing instruments - toy trumpets, simple kazoos, bubbles and balloons. Put a bubble machine in a window where it can blow bubbles in the garden. Watch leaves blowing down on windy days.

### Development Stage 2

## Young children (16-26 months)

Young children's behaviour is affected by the wind, so build this into planning and make sure that on windy days, children have plenty of lively things to do, preferably outside. Make simple kites from plastic carrier bags with the bottoms cut out, or flat bits of black bin bags decorated with a mixture of paint and white glue. Offer streamers and ribbons, flags, bunting and other wind toys in a basket for outdoor play. Try stapling streamers on hats, round fingers, wrists, or ankles.

**Development Stage 3**

## Children (22-40 months)

Explore windy weather by observing clouds, leaves, seeds, even litter blowing around. Look for wind socks, weather vanes and flagpoles in your community. Make wind socks and flags to fly from the top of climbing frames, bushes, fences and trees. Watch what the wind does to hair, clothes, bubbles, feathers, mobiles and wet washing. Begin to explore moving air indoors by looking at how a bubble machine or a hairdryer works.

**Development Stages 4 and 5**

## Older Children (40-60+ months)

Explore how air is used in hand dryers, tumble driers, extractor fans and cooling fans. Play blowing games such as Blow Football or Flip the Kipper. Make cars and boats with sails and watch them sail over paths and water trays when you blow them. Make a wind sock and a simple rain measure for a weather station. Fix four plastic cups to the ends of two straws and fix these to the top of a stick with a drawing pin so the straws will go round.

**Development Stages 5 and 6**

27

## Light and shadow

Shadows fascinate children. Take advantage of the sun when it comes to explore this feature of nature. Does everything have a shadow - even a spider? Can you catch a shadow or change its shape?

Have some fun with the children as you explore together how light and shadow work.

### Young babies (0-11 months)

Look at light and shadow together by walking in day light, artificial light and shadowy places. Switch lights on and off, cover both your heads with a piece of light fabric to explore shadows in a little tent. Make shadow plays with your hands on a wall, look at shadows on the ceiling. Use a spotlight to cast teddy shadows on a wall. Get a baby lamp with a cut-out shadow shade that moves round throwing shadows on the walls and ceiling.

**Development Stage 1**

### Babies (8-20 months)

Look for toys with lights that go on when you push or pull them. Try some battery powered spinning globes, dice and balls. Look for toys with switches and buttons that light up or go on and off - some toys light up when you speak. Lift babies up to switch on safe light switches or pull bathroom light cords - say on/off/on/off as they switch. Explore light and shadow outside on sunny days. Make dens with sheets and ropes so babies can explore being inside a dark place. Go inside with them.

**Development Stage 2**

## Young children (16-26 months)

Light up dark places with safe camping lanterns and torches. Jump on each others' shadows on the ground. Find shady places on sunny days. Use big cardboard cartons (from washing machines or other household goods) to make dens and houses that children can get inside. An easy to open door (with a string pull or a finger hole) will help them to experience near dark in their own little hideout. Tell stories about night and day.

**Development Stage 3**

## Children (22-40 months)

Talk about night, what happens, night time animals and why we are sometimes scared of the dark. Offer resources for making dens and torches to light them. Look for shadows on walls and floors indoors and out. Take photos of shadows for a guessing game. Let them make big, small, fat and thin shadows with their bodies on paths and walls. Photograph the shadows and make a shadow book.

**Development Stages 4 and 5**

## Older Children (40-60+ months)

Make a simple shadow clock from a stick in a bucket of sand. Use chalk to mark where the shadow is each hour. Talk about what is happening. Make shadow puppets and silhouettes of children's heads by shining a light from one side and projecting their silhouettes on a white sheet. Cut them out and see if you can guess who each one is. Look at books about nocturnal animals and people who work at night. Use coloured gels to make glasses for a different look at life.

**Development Stages 5 and 6**

## Sound

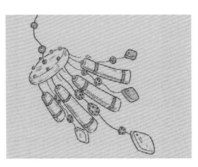

Listening is a vital skill and one that needs support from the earliest age. Make sure the babies and children you work with have plenty of chances to develop their listening skills indoors and outside through naturally occurring sounds and noises.

## Young babies (0-11 months)

Take frequent opportunities to go outside and listen for natural sounds in the garden or street, it only takes a few minutes and will focus babies' attention on natural sounds as well as your own voice.

Stop and listen for birds, the wind, rain on a surface, insects, dogs barking, voices, planes and vehicles passing.

Record some of these familiar sounds and play them at rest time or changing time.

**Development Stage 1**

## Babies (8-20 months)

Hang sound mobiles above changing and rest areas - little bells, shells, small metal objects, coins etc. Make some little shakers from film canisters and rice or little stones. Seal them securely before the vigorous shaking starts! Select toys which make sounds or respond to sounds - shakers and other rattles, cars that whirr, phones that click or ring, toys that talk back or speak when they work.

Use baby gyms with buttons to press and handles to click round.

**Development Stage 2**

## Young children (16-26 months)

Record some familiar sounds - taps, toilets, traffic, animals, children, clocks etc. Take photos of the same objects and play Spot the Sound. Offer a basket of simple musical instruments for outdoor music - have a parade or a procession. Let the children make sound hangings by attaching shells, leaves, cutlery, coins, washers to a wire coat hanger or a piece of string. Hang them in bushes and trees or on a fence.

### Development Stage 3

## Children (22-40 months)

Talk about the sounds that animals and birds make, try imitating them and making a sound picture or rhyme by repeating them or saying them in a pattern.
Use simple musical instruments to echo animal and bird sounds, slithering snakes, hopping frogs, singing birds, flapping wings etc. Move to the music and record the dance in photos or video. Play CDs of natural sounds such as wind, sea and birdsong outside.

### Development Stages 4 and 5

## Older Children (40-60+ months)

Offer a simple tape recorder so children can record sounds indoors and outside, or themselves and other children. Make some noisy toys from recycled materials. Listen for little sounds like clocks ticking, a bee or fly buzzing, whispering, a computer running etc. Play listening games which involve keeping really quiet - such as Grandmother's Footsteps, What's the Time Mr Wolf? or Chinese Whispers. Explore silence as well as sound.

### Development Stages 5 and 6

## Texture and colour

Hundreds of sensory experiences await you out of doors. Whatever the age of the children you work with, the senses of sight and touch are important ones to develop and extend. Children's descriptive and imaginative language is extended and expanded by these activities.

## Young babies (0-11 months)

As you explore the environment out of doors with young babies, help them to touch and feel the world around them. Gently take their hand to textures and surfaces, bring textures to them to touch and feel. Put them on a rug or on the grass, so they can feel the grass and other surfaces. Hold them so their bare feet can touch paving stones, lawns, gravel and sand. This will help to develop the muscles in their feet in preparation for crawling and walking.

**Development Stage 1**

## Babies (8-20 months)

Look carefully at your garden and group room to make sure there are plenty of different textures for babies and children to explore. Concentrate at this stage on the floors and low surfaces - try to include hard, soft, rough and smooth surfaces by adding carpets, fabrics and rugs indoors and sand, gravel, paving, grass and bark in your garden. As babies begin to stand and move around, let them explore safe surfaces in bare feet. This will improve the muscles in their feet and help with walking.

**Development Stage 2**

## Young children (16-26 months)

Explore colour in the garden by sitting or walking with young children and talking about the colours you see together in the sky, in birds, plants and flowers, in clothing, toys and other objects. Model talking about two features - a smooth red bike, a warm blue coat, lumpy brown earth, the fluffy white clouds. Offer lots of different textures in play materials - sand or gravel in dough, stones in sand, paste or ice cubes in water, gloop and slime.

**Development Stage 3**

## Children (22-40 months)

Talk about textures as you work alongside the children. Use a wide vocabulary, not just 'rough' and 'smooth'. Try 'slippery', 'knobbly', 'scratchy', 'uneven', 'ridged', 'bumpy'. Look at the textures of fruit and vegetable skins and other natural objects such as leaves and stones. Make collections of lumpy, smooth, lined, knobbly objects and fabrics.
Add to these with colour collections, maybe linked to a theme or talking table.

**Development Stages 4 and 5**

## Older Children (40-60+ months)

Explore objects that roll, slide, slip, and ones that don't. Experiment with different slopes, slides and surfaces. Explore slippery and gripping shoes and tyres. Begin to talk about shades and different sorts of colours - lime green, dark red, and introduce some new names for colours - what colour is cantaloupe, or sand, or fawn or heliotrope? Get some paint colour shade samples from a DIY shop and see if they can find exact matches with shades and colours. Paint the home corner!

**Development Stages 5 and 6**

## Smell

The perfumes, scents and smells of nature are many and varied, from roses to summer rain, from marigolds to manure! The sense of smell is one of our most powerful in reminding us of places and people, and enhancing our experiences. Yet it is also the most neglected sense. Switch children on to their sense of smell by using natural sources and everyday events.

## Young babies (0-11 months)

Use natural and aromatherapy oils for baby massage - for example lavender, camomile, and mandarin are soothing and relaxing, lemon and tea tree will soothe. Pick herbs and other perfumed flowers and put them near the changing bed or the babies' rest area.

When you peel an orange or prepare food for the baby, talk about the smells.

 Take a walk around your setting and talk about the things you can smell.

### Development Stage 1

## Babies (8-20 months)

Plant herbs and other sweet smelling plants low down in your garden, next to lawns of places where babies crawl and toddle, so babies brush against them as they pass. You could even consider a camomile lawn! Make herbal cushions for quiet areas, hang herbs and dried flowers near changing and rest areas. Grow herbs in pots near doors or in hanging baskets so you can snip a few chives or a bit of oregano to put in a pizza or sprinkle on other snacks.

### Development Stage 2

## Young children (16-26 months)

Mix aromatherapy oils in dough, slime, gloop, sand or paint for a smelly experience. Make ginger biscuits or lemon cakes, spicy samosas or peppermint creams so children can smell food flavourings. Float leaves from lemon thyme, orange peel or lavender in warm water to release the perfumes. Use perfumed candles (in safe holders) to enhance story or group times. When you go out on walks or visits don't forget to talk about the scents and smells you experience.

### Development Stage 3

## Children (22-40 months)

Have some 'smell jars' - small jars or film canisters. Put a small wad of cotton wool inside and add a few drops of the 'smell' - mild disinfectant, lavender oil, herbs, curry powder, perfume, bubble bath. Cover with thin fabric and secure with an elastic band. Let the children sniff and guess.
let the children plant seeds or cuttings of perfumed plants for a sensory garden. Add plants with interesting textures and colours of foliage, seeds and flowers.

### Development Stages 4 and 5

## Older Children (40-60+ months)

Go on a 'smelling walk' and see how many smells you can collect. Go in different buildings or different rooms in your setting and see if they smell different. Make a list of nice and nasty smells and talk about different choices. Have a blindfold challenge with smelling jars (see previous stage) and see who can guess the smell when they can't see in the pot. Make your own pot pourri by collecting flower petals and perfumed leaves and adding essential oils. Or grow lavender for lavender bags.

### Development Stages 5 and 6

## Weather

The weather is a major topic of conversation for adults, but we are often reluctant to give children first hand experiences of different sorts of weather. Many come to your setting by car and spend most of their waking time indoors. Go out and share the weather with babies and children of all ages.

## Young babies (0-11 months)

Just a little walk in the wind, rain, sun or snow will be enough for very young babies. Once they are a bit older, they will begin to enjoy the feel of the weather - the wind ruffling their hair, the rain on their skin, snowflakes on their sleeves.

Try going for a little outing in the garden with one baby under an umbrella big enough for both of you. Transparent umbrellas are fascinating for babies.

### Development Stage 1

## Babies (8-20 months)

Go out every day! How will children learn about the weather if they only experience it through a window? Make sure babies are well waterproofed because they <u>will</u> sit down and they <u>will</u> lie down. Let them explore independently as much as you can, so they see what different surfaces and objects feel like in different weathers. Protection from the sun with sun screen and a hat will ensure they don't get burned.

### Development Stage 2

## Young children (16-26 months)

Look at the weather before the children go outside. Talk about what they need to wear and help with boots and coats if they need them. Plan different equipment and toys for different weathers. Try offering small brooms, buckets, dustpans and window scrapers in wet weather, kites and streamers for the wind, den building stuff for cold days and pop up tents for shade in the sun. Remember children get cold quickly if they don't keep moving.

**Development Stage 3**

## Children (22-40 months)

Make sure the children always have access to outdoor clothing and footwear and they learn early now to put them on. Let children choose the sorts of toys and equipment they need to suit the weather - you could store the equipment in suitable ways to help their choice - a series of bags with stuff for windy, snowy, wet and sunny days (with a picture clue on each to help identify them). Collect weather songs to sing outside, and a list of stories about the weather.

**Development Stages 4 and 5**

## Older Children (40-60+ months)

Try a simple weather chart with symbols and simple words. This could have a suggestion of the sort of clothing children will need for playing outside on that day. Have a TV weather station - a big box with a window cut in one side so a child can look out and present the weather, giving advice on clothing and safety tips for wet, sunny or frosty days. Collect information over a week and talk about the weather you have had. Look back at last week and compare data.

**Development Stages 5 and 6**

## Reflection

Reflections are natural features which hold intense interest for children. Like shadows, they are a new perspective on people and objects, a perspective which can change the shape, form and appearance of everyday and familiar things. Children will be entranced as they use light and reflections to explore and learn first hand.

## Young babies (0-11 months)

Hang CDs above prams and baby chairs, where they can reflect light into the room or sunlight outside. Hold babies so they can see their reflections (and yours) in puddles, in windows, in ice and in shiny metal.
Offer babies unbreakable mirrors with easy hand grips so they can see themselves. Put an unbreakable mirror on the wall next to the changing bed, so babies can see themselves as you change them.

### Development Stage 1

## Babies (8-20 months)

If you have a pond or lake nearby, take a walk to feed the ducks and look at reflections in the water. Put plenty of mirrors so babies can see themselves and their friends. Put them low down on walls, on ceilings above changing tables, hanging in play areas. Offer unbreakable hand mirrors so babies can hold them to see themselves. Talk about reflections as you sit with or hold babies. Look for other reflections in windows, glass doors, metal trays and other reflective surfaces.

### Development Stage 2

## Young children (16-26 months)

Offer full length mirrors in role play areas and mirrors on walls above the play furniture. Place mirrors above sinks in cloakrooms and even on the fronts of cupboards. How about a mirror over the top of every child's peg, to reinforce a sense of self? Don't forget to put unbreakable mirrors outside too. Big wall mirrors, mirrors on the ground, mirror mobiles to reflect the sun and even distorting mirrors for a different look at life.

**Development Stage 3**

## Children (22-40 months)

Cover card shapes with silver or coloured foil to make shiny reflective surfaces. Use these outside to make patterns with leaves, seeds, pebbles or glass beads. Go for a reflecting walk and notice reflections in shop windows and doors, metal surfaces and objects. Take photos of the reflections and talk about what children notice about differences in the reflections. Make the photos into a book and collect mirror pictures for the cover.

**Development Stages 4 and 5**

## Older Children (40-60+ months)

Make a collection of reflective objects and look at the differences in reflections. Use a big mirror to explore what happens when you lift one arm (the reflection will appear to lift the other one). Try doing something simple like putting a coin in a cup while looking at your reflection. Write your names then look at them in a mirror - what has happened? Can the children do mirror writing - probably some of them already do!

**Development Stages 5 and 6**

## Other titles in the Baby and Beyond series include:

* Messy Play * The Sensory World * Sound and Music * Construction * Mark Making * Dolls and Soft Toys * Bikes, Prams and Pushchairs * Finger Play and Rhymes

* Role Play * Food and Cooking * Dens and Shelters * Counting * Small World Play * Tell me a Story * Movement and Beat * Going Out